ALCOHOL

Kirsten Lamb

HODDER
Wayland

an imprint of Hodder Children's Books

© 2001 White-Thomson Publishing Ltd

White-Thomson Publishing Ltd,
2-3 St Andrew's Place, Lewes,
East Sussex BN7 1UP

Published in Great Britain in 2001 by Hodder Wayland, an imprint of Hodder Children's Books.

This book was produced for White-Thomson Publishing Ltd by Ruth Nason.

Design: Carole Binding
Picture research: Glass Onion Pictures

The right of Kirsten Lamb to be identified as the author of this work has been asserted by her in accordance with the Copyright, Designs and Patents Act 1988.

British Library Cataloguing in Publication Data
Lamb, Kirsten
  Alcohol. - (Health Issues)
  1. Alcoholism
  2. Alcohol - Physiological effect
  3. Alcohol - Health aspects
  I. Title
  613.8'1
ISBN 0 7502 3345 1

Printed in Italy by G. Canale & C.S.p.A.

Hodder Children's Books
A division of Hodder Headline Limited
338 Euston Road, London NW1 3BH

Acknowledgements
The author and publishers thank the following for their permission to reproduce photographs and illustrations: Corbis Images: pages 4t (John-Marshall Mantel), 5t (Charles O'Rear), 5b (Macduff Everton), 7t (Franz-Marc Frei), 10 (Ron Slenzak), 13 (Underwood and Underwood), 15 (Steve Chenn), 24 (Rykoff Collection), 28 (James P. Blair), 29 (Adam Woolfit), 31 (Mark L. Stephenson), 43 (Owen Franken), 45 (David H. Wells); Angela Hampton Family Life Pictures: pages 7b, 11, 19, 32, 47; Robert Harding: pages 42, 58t; Impact Photos: pages 14t (Martin Black), 14b (Andy Johnstone), 22 (Geraint Lewis), 25 (Andy Johnstone), 27 (Mike McQueen), 36 (Eliza Armstrong), 50 (Giles Barnard); Nason Publishing: page 40 (C. J. Binding); Photofusion: cover and pages 1 and 37 (Emma Smith), 52 (S. Scott-Hunter); Popperfoto: pages 4b, 33; Science Photo Library: pages 56 (Pascal Goetgheluck), 58b (Hank Morgan); Tony Stone Images: page 49 (Frank Siteman); Topham: pages 51, 54; Wayland Picture Library: pages 12, 41. The illustrations on pages 8, 9, 17, 21, 26, 35 and 39 were drawn by Carole Binding. The 'Six Cs' on page 59 are quoted with the permission of NACOA.

Contents

1 Alcohol Pleasures and dangers

What is alcohol? Is it the 'demon drink' or a pleasant beverage that can be used to good effect? We will try to explore the differences. The aim of this book is to look at the effects of alcohol consumption on individuals and society. Understanding what alcohol is and the pleasures and dangers that drinking can bring helps us to develop the skills to drink in ways that are acceptable to ourselves and to the people around us.

Good and bad
Alcohol can help you relax at a social event. But drinking alcohol to excess can lead to aggression and violence.

Wine and whisky

(Left) Pumping over the wine in a fermentation tank gets the skins and juice of the grapes to mix better. (Below) Stills at a whisky distillery.

So what is alcohol?

Alcoholic drinks contain a chemical called ethanol, which is made by fermentation. The process involves converting sugar to ethanol using an enzyme (called zymase) present in yeast. The sugars used to make alcoholic drinks come from a variety of sources. For example, wine production uses the sugar from grapes. Other drinks are made using potatoes, rice, corn or other cereals. Drinks made by simple fermentation, such as beer and wine, contain up to a maximum of about 12 per cent alcohol. This is a measure of the total amount of alcohol per volume in the drink.

A process called distillation is used to increase the concentration of alcohol in a drink. The first recorded distillation was in the 10th century, by an Arabian physician. Distilling produces stronger alcoholic drinks known as spirits. If the process is allowed to continue for too long, all the impurities in the drink, which add distinctive flavour, are removed and a solution of pure alcohol remains (100 per cent alcohol). The alcohol content of spirits such as whisky, vodka and brandy is 38-45 per cent. Liqueurs and sweetened and flavoured spirits contain 20-40 per cent alcohol.

Mood-altering and intoxicating

Alcohol is a mood-altering substance: when we drink, alcohol enters our brain and affects the chemicals there, and this changes the way we feel and the way we respond to the world around us. The general effect depends on the amount that we drink and the state of mind we are in. Alcohol is also an intoxicating substance: this means that if we drink to excess, alcohol becomes toxic or poisonous to us.

'My friends and I, all girls, are going on holiday soon. I've heard the clubs are fantastic. I'm not much good at dancing or chatting up the lads but it's easier after a drink or two. It's great on holiday. You don't have to get up for work the next day so you can just sleep it off.' (Vicky, 19)

Generally speaking, at low levels of intake, alcohol makes us feel good. It is mood-enhancing. After a couple of drinks we tend to feel less shy, more sociable and more self-confident. In a social context, it is easier to chat and feel happy. We can lose some of our inhibitions and feel strong and more able to face challenges.

As we drink more alcohol, it starts to have a depressant effect, slowing down the brain's activity. First our judgement becomes impaired. We are less able to perform fine tasks accurately. We are also dangerously unaware of the effect the drink is having on our performance. We still believe that we are totally in control. This may tempt us to do things that are not safe, like driving a car. Our coordination becomes impaired and we become clumsy. We may knock things over or fall. We may lose our sexual inhibitions and do things that we later regret. The more we drink, the more 'drunk' we become. We lose control of ourselves, may become violent and are often extremely antisocial. When we sober up we may have no recollection of the state we were in.

'It's embarrassing going out drinking with Gavin. He never knows when to stop. His voice gets louder and he argues with everyone about anything. We have to hold him up to walk him home. Then he doesn't remember anything about it and does the same thing the next week.' (Rick, 18)

Gradually, with more alcohol, our brain activity becomes more depressed and our level of consciousness is reduced. At this stage, alcohol affects us almost like a general

anaesthetic (for putting a patient to sleep before an operation). We may lapse into unconsciousness and coma. During an alcohol-induced coma, a person may have fits. Commonly, vomiting occurs. Vomiting when unconscious is dangerous. We can inhale vomit into our lungs and may then die from asphyxiation. There are other dangers. As consciousness is lost, it is common for people to fall. Falls can cause injury, most seriously to the head. So the final complication of acute alcohol poisoning is death.

Sleeping it off

Drinking too much can make you very drowsy.

Remembering Michael

My son Michael was 20 when he died. He was a great rugby player. They had just won the cup. The celebrations afterwards were apparently really good. After a big team dinner they went on to the clubs in town. His friends told me that he had a lot to drink. There were toasts at the dinner and he carried on drinking at the club. At about one in the morning they lost sight of him and presumed that he had decided to go home. That's just what he did. No one saw him leave. He got home and managed to get upstairs to his first floor flat. But he obviously fell at the top and crashed all the way down. The next morning his flat mate came back and found him at the bottom of the stairs. The post-mortem examination found that he had died from massive head injuries, but his blood alcohol level was sky high. He wasn't a bad lad. He just went too far one time too often. He had reason to celebrate but just went too far. I miss him so terribly.

Alcohol absorption

When we drink alcohol it is absorbed rapidly from the small intestine into our bloodstream. The speed at which it is absorbed depends on:

- whether we are male or female – blood alcohol levels rise faster in women
- our body weight
- whether we have food in our stomachs. If we drink on an empty stomach the effects of alcohol occur more quickly. Conversely, fatty food in the stomach delays the absorption of alcohol.

As we consume alcohol, the amount of alcohol in our blood (measured in milligrams per 100 millilitres) rises steadily. The highest level of alcohol in the blood occurs about one hour after drinking.

The effect of blood alcohol (mg/100ml) on an average drinker

mg/100ml

20	Feeling good. Little or no effect on performance.
40	Able to 'let go' socially. Slightly dangerous when driving fast.
60	Judgement impaired. Incapable of making important decisions. Driving becoming reckless.
80	Definite loss of coordination. Unsafe at any speed.
100	Tendency to lose sexual control, if not too sleepy. Knocking over drinks.
160	Obviously drunk. Possibly aggressive. Unmanageable. May have later loss of memory of events.
300	Often spontaneously incontinent. Barely rousable. May be in a coma.
500	Liable to die without medical attention.

Blood alcohol levels (mg/100ml) after:

Units	1 hour man	1 hour woman	2 hours man	2 hours woman	3 hours man	3 hours woman
1	20	30	0	10	0	0
2	40	60	10	20	0	10
3	60	80	30	40	20	30
4	80	110	60	80	40	60
5	100	140	80	110	60	80
6	120	170	100	140	90	120
7	140	200	120	170	110	140

♂ man ♀ woman ♂ man ♀ woman ♂ man ♀ woman

Young people and alcohol

Many studies in the UK have looked at young people's drinking habits. In the 16-24 age group, 79 per cent of men said they had been drunk in the last 3 months and 32 per cent that they had been drunk at least once per week; 68 per cent of women said they had been drunk in the last 3 months and 17 per cent that they had been drunk at least once per week. Research and observations from hospital accident and emergency units in the UK estimate that about 1,000 children under the age of 15 are admitted to hospital every year with acute alcohol poisoning.

How can you try to prevent disasters when you and your friends are out drinking? The answer is to look out for each other. If one of your group becomes very drunk, try to stop them from drinking more and get them to a safe place where they can be looked after until they sober up. Most problems with alcohol intoxication are caused by the effect of unconsciousness on our ability to breathe properly and to keep our airway open so that oxygen can get into our lungs. The other problems are associated with accidents and injuries and with inhalation of vomit.

Blood alcohol levels

This table shows the effect of drinking different amounts of alcohol (units) on the blood alcohol level of average male and female drinkers. A unit of alcohol is equivalent to half a pint of lager or an ordinary glass of wine. (See page 20.)

A party that ended in hospital

Ricky, Jane, Sam and Diane are all fifteen. They have become quite used to drinking. It was Sam's birthday and he had a disco at the village hall. There wasn't supposed to be any alcohol, but Diane's older sister had brought some. Diane was tense. She had been going out with Sam, but she knew she would not have him to herself at his birthday do. She felt more confident after a few drinks. Then she saw Sam dancing with someone else and it looked serious. She decided to go outside with the bottle.

Luckily, a couple of hours later, Jane noticed that Diane wasn't in the hall. She found her slumped on the bench outside and couldn't rouse her. Ricky came and saw Diane as well. They both realized she was unconscious and Jane used her mobile phone to call an ambulance.

What will happen to Diane when the ambulance comes? First the ambulance crew will check her vital functions: they will make sure she is breathing and has a good pulse and blood pressure. She will be taken to the accident department at the hospital, where further tests will be done to check that she is unconscious from alcohol poisoning and not from any other cause. She will be examined carefully to make sure that she did not injure her head when she fell. She may have become very cold whilst slumped unconscious outside, so her body temperature will be checked. Hypothermia (the body's temperature falling too low) can commonly occur.

Emergency
Alcohol intoxication needs emergency care.

The role of the hospital staff is then to look after Diane until she recovers. They must make sure that:

- no more alcohol is absorbed. Sometimes the stomach is washed out to prevent further alcohol absorption. A tube is passed through the patient's mouth into the stomach, with the patient lying on their side. Water is poured down the tube to induce vomiting of the stomach contents.

- breathing is maintained. Sometimes, the patient needs help with breathing and has to be artificially ventilated. A tube is passed through the patient's mouth into their upper airway – the trachea. This tube is attached to a pumping machine that allows the lungs to expand and contract and fill with air.

- vomiting (if it occurs) does not obstruct the airway.

- dehydration does not occur. Sometimes fluids are given into a vein by an intravenous infusion.

- hypothermia does not develop. The patient is slowly warmed and their temperature monitored.

- blood sugar levels are maintained. They can fall very low in alcohol intoxication. Glucose may need to be given in an intravenous drip.

If all goes well, most people recover within 24 hours. They are often left with a 'hangover', with a headache and dry mouth and feeling irritable and tired.

The change of state from drunk to unconscious can happen very quickly as we take in more alcohol. Being aware of how much we are drinking and the effects that the alcohol is having on us can help to protect us.

An ABC

If your friend becomes unconscious, some basic first aid and common sense may save their life.

A – stands for airway – keep it open

B – stands for breathing – make sure your friend is breathing

C – stands for circulation – make sure your friend has a pulse

Call the ambulance – dial 999 and tell the ambulance control officer what has happened and where you are.

Hangover

The after-effects of too much alcohol are a dry mouth, irritability and a headache.

2 Attitudes to alcohol
Uses and benefits

It is likely that alcohol has been an important part of human life for many thousands of years. Ancient Egyptian tombs and papyri show evidence of wine consumption and many great Roman writers describe wine-growing in Italy. As the power of the Romans spread north through Europe, they took wine-making with them. In medieval Europe, wine-making was often the preserve of monasteries.

Medieval tavern
People have been drinking alcohol for pleasure and in each other's company for hundreds of years.

In Shakespeare's England, in the seventeenth century, alcohol was commonly produced in rural areas. Beer was made from barley, cider from apples and perry from pears. Beer was the staple drink of men, women and children before the arrival of clean water, tea and coffee as alternatives. Drinking became a sociable activity with the development of inns.

Gin Lane
An eighteenth-century view of the effects of gin.

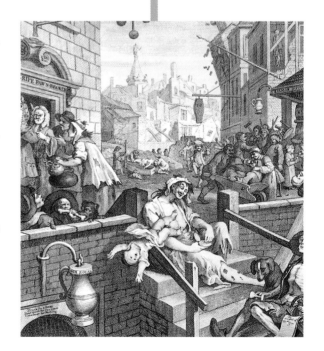

Inevitably, along with the consumption of alcohol came drunkenness. In eighteenth-century Britain attempts were made to control it by closing public houses on Sundays. In England, as the eighteenth century progressed, there was greater access to alcohol of higher strength than beer and ale. Gin became the drink of the people. Drunkenness and excessive expenditure on drink were seen as major evils of city life. The government tried to control the consumption of gin by limiting the places at which it could be bought and raising taxation on it.

In the nineteenth century the Temperance movement developed. It was linked to non-conformist religious groups. Individuals swore an oath to stay teetotal (never to drink any alcohol). At the same time, alternative entertainments to drinking were becoming more usual, including music, reading, theatre-going and holidays at the seaside. Entertainment was needed to counteract the tedium and hard work of life.

In the USA in the twentieth century, fear of the effects of alcohol on society led to the passing of the 18th amendment to the constitution. During the period of Prohibition (1920-33), the making, transport and sale of alcoholic drinks were forbidden throughout the USA. The aim was to reduce drunkenness, violence and accidents at work. The effect was to drive alcohol production and drinking 'underground'. Bars developed in basements, at the back of shops and in libraries. The 'speakeasy' or illicit liquor shop became part of American life. Gangland battles over the illegal production and sale of alcohol became common.

Illegal ale
During Prohibition, the police poured away illegally made alcohol.

Now, in the twenty-first century, alcohol is tolerated by most societies. It is only Islamic law that prohibits the use of alcohol altogether. All other cultures, religions and societies accept it. However, there are groups who prefer to prohibit alcohol use for various reasons.

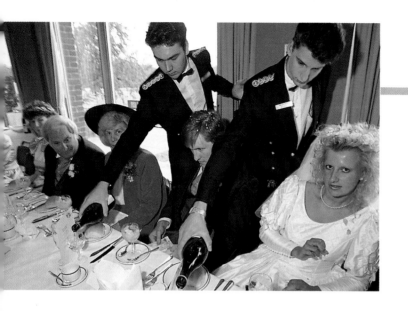

Celebration

There are many events in our society where alcohol is used in a positive way. Alcohol is a central part of many ceremonies.

Drinking styles

Within societies, acceptable drinking styles vary considerably. What one group considers acceptable and normal may be seen as outrageous by another. Similarly, the context in which we drink varies. So we need to learn the acceptability of different drinking behaviours in different contexts. Furthermore, we are all different as individuals. We must learn the effect that

Winston and his parents

Winston is a Jamaican 20 year-old. He likes to go down to the bars by the beach with his friends. There, he drinks rum. It is readily available. He enjoys the way he feels after a few drinks and knows he dances better then to the loud music. His parents, Rita and Wesley, live out of town and are devout churchgoers. They really disapprove of his drinking behaviour. They just stay confident that he will grow out of it as his responsibilities change.

Weekending

Groups of young people often binge drink on a Friday night.

alcohol has on us, and what we as individuals find pleasurable and acceptable. Our drinking style changes through our life as our circumstances change. To sum up, the consumption of alcohol is a complex behaviour that is modified by all sorts of factors.

When young people start experimenting with alcohol they are at the first stages of developing the skills of drinking in a way that is acceptable to themselves and to others. Drinking usually starts at home but as teenagers become more independent they increasingly drink outside the home. Peak ages of alcohol consumption are usually between 16 and 24. As young people gain responsibilities, their consumption falls.

Sometimes people get it wrong. They do not work out in advance what is an acceptable way to drink in a given situation. People who persistently get it wrong can become labelled by society as 'problem drinkers'.

'Old uncle Jack came on his own to our wedding. During the dancing, it became obvious that he had quietly gone too far with his drinking. He was slouched over his table, leaning on the starched table cloth and snoring noisily, much to everyone's embarrassment.'

Jane and Dean

Jane is 25. She and Dean have been married for a couple of years. Last year baby Lauren was born. Jane remembers when she was a student and went out drinking with her friends. Often she drank so much that the next day she couldn't really remember much that had happened. At the time it was a good laugh but she wouldn't want to go back to that life. When she and Dean got married they were both just starting in good jobs. They decided that they wanted to start a family young. Now, occasionally Dean stops for a quick drink with friends on the way home from work but usually the only alcohol is a drink with meals and only really at the weekend.

Wine and dine
Mixed groups drink differently from all males or all females together.

Health benefits

In recent years studies have provided evidence of a relationship between moderate alcohol consumption and health benefit. It seems that people who drink as little as one small alcoholic drink per day gain some health benefit.

The major area where there seems to be proof of benefit is in protection against coronary heart disease. Coronary heart disease is thought to be caused by the narrowing of major blood vessels when cholesterol is deposited on their walls. This narrowing of blood vessels reduces the amount of oxygen transported to the muscle of the heart, which then gets damaged. This is what happens in a heart attack. The cholesterol deposited on the blood vessel walls also contributes to blood-clotting, which narrows the blood vessels further.

Two beneficial effects of alcohol seem to be that it actively lowers the bad fraction of cholesterol in the blood and raises the useful part of cholesterol; and that it reduces some of the blood-clotting mechanisms. However these benefits are only apparent with small daily amounts of alcohol. Heavy drinking damages the heart. There appears to be a 'J'-shaped curve when level of alcohol consumption is plotted on a graph against risk.

Cholesterol

- Cholesterol is a fat found in the blood.
- There are 2 types: LDL and HDL cholesterol.
- High levels of LDL cholesterol are known to increase the risk of heart disease.
- HDL cholesterol appears to protect against heart disease.
- Cholesterol levels in the blood can be reduced by eating less animal fat and dairy products.
- Fish oils are a good source of HDL cholesterol.

There is confusing evidence about the effects of alcohol consumption on the risk of stroke. Strokes occur when part of the brain becomes damaged, either because it loses its blood supply when the artery to the brain becomes blocked or because of bleeding from the little blood vessels in the brain. It seems that small amounts of alcohol consumption may protect against the first form of stroke but increase the risk of the type of stroke caused by bleeding.

One other area that seems to show some proof of benefit is in the production of gallstones. Gallstones form in the gall bladder and can then irritate it and cause episodes of severe pain. A study of nurses in the USA has concluded that drinking alcohol regularly reduces the risk of forming gallstones.

Many other benefits of some alcohol consumption have been suggested but not proven. These range from lowering the risk of developing diabetes and rheumatoid arthritis to reducing the chances of catching the common cold. It is recognized that the positive mood and sense of wellbeing that drinking can induce can have health benefits but these have not been quantified.

It is important to realize that the benefits of alcohol in relation to the risk of coronary heart disease have only been investigated in people over the age of 40. It is not known whether drinking when young adds to or detracts from those benefits. Probably for young people the potential social harm of drinking outweighs any theoretical health benefit.

The J-shaped curve

This graph shows how the risk of death from various causes differs from the norm (1.0) as alcohol is consumed.

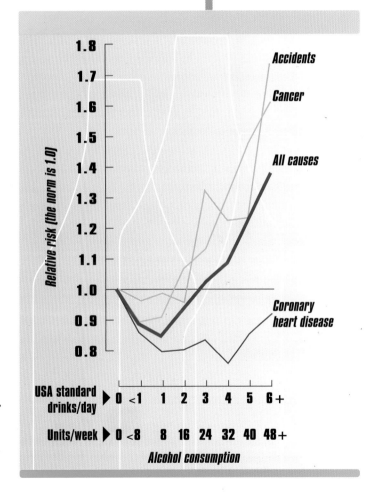

3 Alcohol and young people
Facts and figures

When we drink alcohol, it is rapidly absorbed into our bloodstream and is then carried to all parts of the body including the brain. The liver works hard to break down and remove the alcohol but cannot usually keep pace with what we drink. In an adult it takes one hour for the liver to break down the alcohol in one ordinary-sized drink.

In general, alcohol has a faster and more powerful effect on teenagers than on adult drinkers. The amount of alcohol that gets into your blood – the blood alcohol level – depends on how much you drink but also on your size. Teenagers are usually smaller and lighter than adults. As people become more experienced or regular drinkers, their livers become more efficient at breaking down alcohol. Teenagers are inexperienced drinkers.

Quickly absorbed
Stronger drinks like spirits, and fizzy drinks like champagne and cider, are absorbed into the bloodstream more quickly than others.

The liver
The liver regulates substances in the blood. It:

- keeps blood sugar level constant by storing extra sugar after a meal and releasing sugar between meals.
- makes bile. Bile gets rid of waste products from worn-out red blood cells. It also contains chemicals to help absorb fat from the gut.
- stores spare amino acids for protein-building, spare iron for blood, and vitamins A and D.
- makes many of the proteins found in blood, particularly those needed for blood-clotting.
- metabolizes or breaks down chemicals that are potentially poisonous to the body. This is the effect that the liver has on alcohol and other drugs.

How strong is your drink?

It's important to be aware of how much alcohol you are drinking. The huge array of alcoholic drinks that are available vary considerably in strength (the amount of alcohol they contain) and so in the effect that they have. The amount of alcohol in a drink is usually stated as a percentage of the total volume and written as '% abv' (alcohol by volume).

Low-alcohol drinks are often assumed to be free of alcohol. Don't be taken in. If you drink enough, or mix one of these drinks with other alcoholic drinks, it can have the same effect as a stronger drink. Examples in this group are low-alcohol beer, lager and wine. They average 1% abv.

Moderate-strength drinks include ordinary or special bitter and lager beers. They average 3-4% alcohol.

Stronger than you think! Examples in this group are:

⦿ premium lagers, cider and 'dry' lagers. These average 5-8% alcohol.

⦿ the new alcoholic lemonades, colas and fizzy pops known as alcopops. These average 6% alcohol. They are deceptive because their sweetness masks the taste and strength of the alcohol, making it easy for you to drink more than you can handle.

⦿ most ordinary wines, which average 12-13% alcohol. However wine is normally drunk in smaller volumes than beers and alcopops.

⦿ fortified wines such as Bailey's, Cinzano and Martini. Their alcoholic content is 30%! So, even diluted with mixers, they can have a dramatic effect on you.

Teenagers
Young teenagers often drink very sweet, fizzy alcoholic drinks that are deceptively strong.

The **strongest drinks** are the spirits, including whisky, brandy, rum, vodka and gin. On average they contain 40% alcohol. They are commonly drunk with mixers such as water, lemonade and soda, which makes them more palatable but does not reduce their impact and may increase the speed at which they are absorbed by the body.

Alcohol units

Going by percentages of alcohol in different drinks, it is not very easy to measure how much alcohol you are drinking. To make it easier, in the UK, units of alcohol are used. Guidance is given about how many units it is acceptable and safe to drink. This guidance is given for adults and therefore the amounts would be excessive for teenagers.

1 unit of alcohol is equivalent to:

For men the upper limits are 3-4 units per day.
For women the upper limits are 2-3 units per day.

For adults, the recommended safe limits for alcohol consumption are expressed as a daily amount. It is now recognized that drinking small volumes regularly is much better for us than drinking large volumes once a week or irregularly. The upper limits are amounts known to have no ill effects on health.

half a pint (220 ml) of ordinary strength beer, lager or cider

1 measure (25ml) of spirits

Calculating units

A simple way to calculate units is to multiply the volume of the drink in millilitres by the % abv and divide by 1000. For example, to calculate the units in a 125ml glass of wine of 12% abv:

125 x 12 = 1500 ÷ 1000 = 1.5 units.

1 small glass of wine (9% abv)

Another way of looking at alcohol content in drinks is to look at the number of grams of alcohol present. I UK unit of alcohol contains 8 grams of alcohol.

Different countries use different ways of measuring amounts of alcohol. For example, the USA uses a 'standard drink', which contains 14 grams of alcohol. A standard drink is a 12 oz beer, 5 oz glass of wine or 1.5 oz measure of spirits.

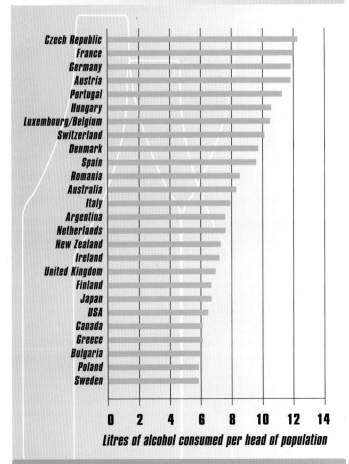

Alcohol consumption per person in one year in leading countries

Litres of alcohol consumed per head of population

Worldwide drinking

The amount of alcohol consumed varies greatly from country to country. So too does the type of alcohol people drink. The UK, Germany, Denmark and the Nordic countries are predominantly beer-drinking, whilst people in southern Europe drink more wine.

The law about drinking alcohol

Most children have their first taste of alcohol between the ages of 8 and 12. By 14-15 years, more than 90 per cent will have tasted alcohol. In most countries, however, it is illegal for teenagers to purchase and sometimes to drink alcohol. The UK law on alcohol consumption says that:

- It is illegal to give alcohol to a child under 5 years.

- Under-14s are not allowed in the bars of licensed premises but can enter other areas where alcohol is consumed, such as eating areas. They are not allowed to drink alcohol in these premises.

- 14-16 year-olds are allowed in to bars of licensed premises but may not buy or consume alcohol there.

- 16-18 year-olds may buy some alcoholic drinks but only to consume with a meal and not to drink at the bar of licensed premises.

- It is illegal for under-18s to buy or drink alcohol on licensed premises except with a meal (as above). It is illegal to sell alcohol to anyone under 18 in a bar. Under-18s are not allowed to work in bars.

- It is an offence to be drunk and disorderly in a public place.

In the park
Some teenagers gather to drink outdoors. It is to hide their drinking from other adults.

Tracy

Tracy is 15. She socializes in a large mixed group of friends from her neighbourhood. Sometimes they go to the youth club but it's not always fun. Sometimes there are other groups there that they don't like. One of the boys got some alcohol from home. His Dad always has cans of beer in and he didn't miss a few. They all go to the little kids' play area in the park and sit on the swings, drinking and chatting. Tracy and the girls find it easy to buy alcohol from the off-licence. It's easy to pass for 18 when you wear make-up. Their parents would be shocked to know what they get up to, so they keep it quiet.

Teenage drinking behaviour

Many factors influence teenage drinking behaviour. If your parents drink alcohol sensibly you are likely to see some of the positive sides of drinking. If there is frequent drunkenness at home, or a very rigid attitude against alcohol consumption, you may have a more negative attitude to experimentation. If all your friends are regular drinkers you are much more likely to do the same than behave differently. Some young people use alcohol to relieve stress, especially if they have seen others use it for that purpose. If you are the sort of person who likes going out regularly, you are likely to come into contact earlier with a drinking culture.

'Dad's always coming home drunk after work. He seems to need to stop at the pub most nights. He's in a foul mood when he gets back. I don't know what I think about drinking. I tend to stay home because I'm worried about Mum.'
(Paul, 15)

Surveys from North America and the UK show that teenagers have little difficulty getting hold of alcohol, despite the fact that it is illegal for them to buy it. How do you feel about that? Teenagers as young as 15-16 seem able to buy alcohol in supermarkets, off-licences and shops. By 17 years many are drinking regularly in pubs and clubs. Many also persuade older people to buy the alcohol for them.

Most teenagers who drink regularly do so at home with their families. As they become more independent, it becomes more likely that they will drink outside the home. They may be quite happy about their drinking behaviour and do so openly with their parents' knowledge, or they may feel guilty and anxious about their parents' reaction. In that case, they may drink furtively.

'At home Dad opens a bottle of wine with dinner. My brother and I are both allowed a small glass. It's quite nice but I reckon it's a bit over-rated.'
(Sophie, 15)

It seems that over the last 20-30 years the number of teenagers who drink regularly has not changed significantly. However the amount that teenagers drink has increased steadily. Boys still drink more than girls, but the amount and frequency of drinking by girls is rising rapidly. By the age of 16-17 years, roughly the same numbers of girls and boys drink heavily. Young adults aged 17-24 are the heaviest drinkers in the population. Girls tend to reduce their consumption again at a slightly younger age than boys. The peak age for girls is 16-18 years and for boys 18-21 years.

Most teenagers who start drinking apparently do so for the thrill of its mood-altering effects – of feeling drunk. Their perception is that alcohol is safer than illegal drugs. Studies from around the world have shown that teenagers deliberately plan to binge drink, particularly on special occasions such as birthdays and end-of-term parties. Most teenagers who binge drink do not see it as risky behaviour. They consider it socially better and wiser than drinking small amounts regularly. But there are problems with this sort of drinking behaviour and the drunkenness it causes:

- feeling sick and vomiting
- feeling dizzy and faint
- falls, because of feeling dizzy and uncoordinated
- alcohol intoxication (much more likely to occur in teenagers because of alcohol's faster and more powerful effect on young people)
- hangover. As the brain recovers from the effects of alcohol it is common to feel sick and irritable, with a headache and dry mouth.
- accidents, including those caused by drink-driving, being injured as a drunk pedestrian, drowning, accidents at home and injuries as a result of violence.
- violence. Alcohol and aggression are closely linked. It is commoner to be violent, and to be assaulted, when drunk.
- involvement in criminal behaviour. Reasons for convictions of young people related to alcohol include

The morning after
A French postcard from the 1920s pictured a hangover.

disorderly behaviour, purchasing alcohol illegally and violence when drunk.

- feelings of guilt and sadness, which sometimes lead as far as attempting suicide.

- poor concentration after the event, which can have a negative effect on school performance.

- risky sexual behaviour. Many young people, especially girls, report that they were under the influence of alcohol when they first had sex. Condoms and other forms of contraception are used less carefully by those who are drunk and so the risk of both pregnancy and sexually transmitted infection increases.

- inability to perform sexually. Many young men report being unable to sustain an erection when drunk.

- using other drugs. Those who drink heavily are more likely than non-drinkers to be smokers. It is sometimes suggested that drinking and smoking lead young people into other drug-taking behaviour. It is certainly true that those who drink heavily are more likely than those who do not drink to be in situations where other drugs are available.

Alcohol and smoking
Bars and clubs where young people go to drink are often smoking zones.

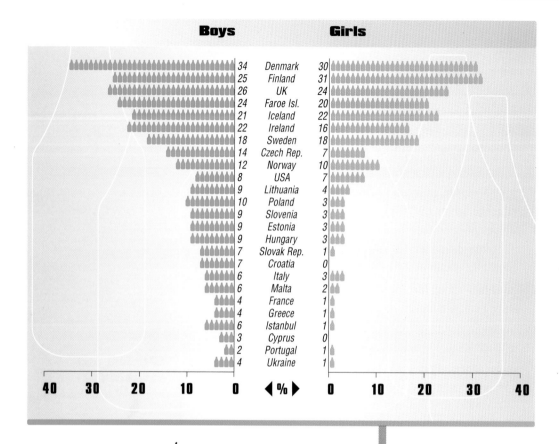

	Boys			Girls
	34	Denmark	30	
	25	Finland	31	
	26	UK	24	
	24	Faroe Isl.	20	
	21	Iceland	22	
	22	Ireland	16	
	18	Sweden	18	
	14	Czech Rep.	7	
	12	Norway	10	
	8	USA	7	
	9	Lithuania	4	
	10	Poland	3	
	9	Slovenia	3	
	9	Estonia	3	
	9	Hungary	3	
	7	Slovak Rep.	1	
	7	Croatia	0	
	6	Italy	3	
	6	Malta	2	
	4	France	1	
	4	Greece	1	
	6	Istanbul	1	
	3	Cyprus	0	
	2	Portugal	1	
	4	Ukraine	1	

40   30   20   10   0   ◀ % ▶   0   10   20   30   40

Why do teenagers drink?

Young people drink for many of the same reasons as people of all ages, but there are also some reasons that are specific to teenagers.

- Drinking in a social context is seen as important to help relaxation and reduce inhibitions. If friends are regular drinkers, young people often wish to match them and get their approval.

- Young people enjoy the mood-altering effects of alcohol. Many say that they drink in order to get drunk and feel the 'buzz' that alcohol gives them.

- For most young people drinking is used when going out and to have a good time. It is a fun thing to do.

- The consumption of alcohol is often a consequence of the place where teenagers meet to socialize – often pubs, bars and clubs.

Drunkenness

The proportions of boys and girls who had been drunk ten times or more in one year.

◉ It is often easy to feel constrained by the boundaries that school and home impose. The altered behaviour that drinking induces can feel like a release from those constraints.

◉ Fashion and trends encourage teenagers to drink and influence what they drink.

◉ Leisure activities for young people are very varied. Drinking alcohol can be part of a young person's leisure activities, as much as going to music events or taking part in sport.

Increasingly young people are looking at the range of possibilities for altering mood in different settings. Alcohol is often used, but other, illicit drugs may nowadays be used in its place.

The majority of teen-agers who drink use alcohol in a sensible way and get pleasure from it for most of the time, although on occasions the boundaries are broken. However, there are some groups of teenagers who always drink in a way that is both antisocial and potentially harmful to themselves.

New Year
The 'buzz' of alcohol may help you to party into the New Year.

The important thing about alcohol consumption at any age is to be aware of how alcohol affects you as an individual. If you then know what you are drinking and how much alcohol it contains, and if you understand the settings in which you drink and the reasons why you are drinking, you should finally stay safe.

4 Why we drink
Pressures and choices

In the community in which you live there are many pressures on you to participate in all sorts of behaviours. Let's look at some of the influences on drinking patterns.

Family pressures

As children, we see life mainly through the eyes of our family. The three examples here show how our home environment can affect us, sometimes positively and sometimes negatively.

At home
You are bound to be influenced by your parents' attitude to alcohol and by your experience of alcohol at home.

The Smiths

Emily and Jack Smith are 16 and 14 respectively and live with their parents. Mr Smith works full-time in the bank. Mrs Smith has a part-time job and is often able to work from home. Emily and Jack are a lively pair with many groups of friends at school, sports clubs and so on. Emily is allowed to go out and about with her friends but her parents like to know where she is, what time she will be home and how she plans to get home. They are flexible if she rings to tell them what is happening. They don't mind her having a drink but do disapprove of drunkenness. They, themselves, enjoy having friends round and sharing a bottle of wine. Emily and Jack also disapprove of getting drunk and avoid the groups that drink heavily.

Cathy and Fred

Cathy and her older brother Fred come from a strict family that is very religious. Their parents strongly disapprove of alcohol and have been teetotal for many years since they joined their church. Alcohol is banned at home. Nowadays Fred, who is 18, is hardly allowed home. He sometimes sees his mother for short periods but his father won't talk to him. He got involved with a bad lot and from the age of 16 was regularly drunk. He has had a conviction for driving when drunk. Cathy is confused. She has never tried alcohol and doesn't like the thought of it. But she does find the rigid views at home very oppressive at times and feels she understands why her brother did what he did.

Fiona and Leonie

Fiona and Leonie have had a difficult time. They were aware from a young age that their father often came home drunk. He was very loud and sometimes aggressive. He never hit them, but they knew he hurt their mother because they saw the bruises, although she tried to hide them. Now they are older they can see the effect this has had on them. There were times when they were teenagers that their parents were so preoccupied with their own problems that Fiona and Leonie did what they liked. They experimented with getting drunk themselves. Now the family is still together and the girls reckon they have learnt to cope with a great deal over the years.

Peer-group pressure

Your peer group are the people of the same age and situation as yourself. There may be just one group of friends that you spend time with, or you may have one group of friends at school but mix with a different group for sporting activities and another group in your neighbourhood. Within any group of friends we are both influenced by the feelings and attitudes of the others and have the power to influence them ourselves.

In relation to alcohol consumption, it seems that if you are a regular drinker you will mix with others who are also regular drinkers. It tends to be true

Beer festival
Like-minded people come together for a beer festival.

Leader of the gang

Darren is the loudest member of our gang. I've seen what he really gets up to so I don't always believe all he says, but some of the girls who fancy him are really impressed. He says that his Dad lets him have a whisky at home and that he can carry his drink well. I've seen him in the pub choking on a glass of spirits and I've seen him really drunk! He also claims to have had sex with a number of girls already and says it's really cool to smoke. I did overhear Laura and her friends saying to each other that he would think they were real wimps if they didn't smoke and drink. I saw them all giggling outside the shop, working out how to buy a packet of fags. Laura is dead keen to impress Darren. It's a shame that one person has so much power, especially when most of what he brags about isn't even true! (Jason, 17)

that we feel most comfortable in a group of people who like the same things as we do. However, myths can develop within groups, as Jason's description of Darren shows.

Pressures from the alcohol industry

The alcohol industry in the Western world is a powerful force. In the mid-1990s, in the UK, the drinks market was worth £26 billion. It employed nearly 300,000 people. All the large alcohol companies were ranked in the top 100 companies in the country. Not only does the alcohol industry earn vast sums of money from sales, but so does the government. All alcoholic drinks are taxed. The income that the UK government earned from alcohol sales by taxation in the mid-1990s was over 5 per cent of total government income.

In order to maintain profits, the alcohol industry is keen to keep up levels of consumption. In the mid-1990s, the alcohol industry in the UK spent £115 million on advertising. Advertising is usually targeted on specific groups of people. It is logical to assume that such vast sums of money would not be spent on advertising unless it was recognized as a powerful force in encouraging us to consume. Studies have shown that rising expenditure on

advertising *is* associated with an increase in consumption and conversely that advertising bans are linked with a reduction in consumption.

There is dispute about whether the alcohol industry specifically develops drinks to be attractive to young people and targets them in its advertising and marketing. There is evidence from the USA that magazines with a large youth readership include high levels of advertising for alcohol and cigarettes. Young people often like and recall alcohol advertising. The advertisers are clever at making their ideas attractive and snappy. Trendy young people are used in the adverts. The most popular ones are usually funny and are often involved with sport. However, young people are very aware of the difference between enjoying the adverts – their characters, humour, music, etc – and approving of the product. Teenagers are perfectly able to make up their own minds and make their own judgement about whether to respond to the advert.

Not only does the alcohol industry advertise its products extensively, but also it markets them carefully, keeping up to date with trends and fashions. The outlets where alcohol can be bought and consumed are changing. The

'In' places
Modern themed bars and restaurants are quite different from the all-male drinking establishments of the past.

simple drinking establishments of the past have been replaced with a wide variety of places where you can drink and take advantage of extra services on offer, such as eating, sporting activities, and venues for parties or for bands to perform. Other techniques are used to attract us, such as holding theme evenings or quiz nights to pull in different types of people. The old male preserve of the bar has changed and women and younger people too are attracted to places where alcohol is on offer.

New types of drinks are developed, following trends and fashions, as the industry tries to expand the numbers and types of people who are drinking. The industry also tries to increase public awareness of its products through sports promotion. This has many advantages as well as disadvantages. It may encourage young people to drink, but it also gives financial backing to the sports that young people enjoy, thereby creating more chances to both watch and participate.

Jerry

I used to drink regularly and often got drunk. I've been involved in fights because of it. My heavy drinking bouts were usually at the weekend, so I nearly always had a hangover at the beginning of the week. I felt awful, had a headache and couldn't concentrate. It all seemed OK and a laugh till things started to go wrong. I knew I could have got better exam results. My girlfriend dumped me. Sex was hopeless. I was usually too drunk. We were always arguing. My skin was awful and I was developing a beer gut. My sports trainer took me aside. He told me I'd be a total failure if I didn't sort myself out. I really wanted to do something with sport, either playing or training. So I've stopped drinking and started a training routine. I'm really pleased with myself because I look good, feel good and know that I can go places now.

Looking ahead
Actress Drew Barrymore needed treatment for alcohol dependence when she was only 14. Since then she has been fine and is determined to continue that way.

Making up your own mind

With the right knowledge and information and personal skills, you can use alcohol in the way that is right for you. You may choose not to drink at all. Drinking sensibly has many advantages.

It's hard to be as disciplined as Jerry. So how do you try to resist all the pressures?

- You may think that you are the only person amongst your friends who doesn't want to drink. Check it out because you may not be right. There is support in numbers.

- If your friends are real friends, you should be able to trust them not to laugh at you but to support you in your decision. If they won't, are they real friends?

- Know your own reasons for not drinking and believe in them. For example, you may not like feeling out of control. If you are confident about this you will respect yourself more and feel good. Then you won't need the extra buzz that alcohol gives.

⦿ If people have told you that drinking relaxes you and boosts your confidence, remember that there are other ways to do the same thing. Relaxation techniques and other relaxing activities like yoga may help. Participating in sport will make you feel good. Exercise can relax you. Finding ways of talking about the things that are troubling you, rather than trying to drown them in alcohol, will also help.

⦿ If you are worried that you may be drinking too much, or concerned that one of your friends is, find ways of obtaining information to help you. Read about alcohol abuse by using your local library. Surf the Web for information. Talk to people you know, such as teachers, doctors, counsellors, youth leaders and perhaps relatives. There are also telephone helplines that you can ring for confidential advice.

⦿ You may be out socializing with friends who drink. How do you stick to your decision either not to drink at all or to drink sensibly? It is wise to know about the different types of alcohol available and choose lower-alcohol alternatives. Drink slowly. Make one drink last as long as 2 or 3 that your friends are drinking. Drink soft drinks between alcoholic drinks.

'You can make one drink go further and last longer by diluting it with a soft drink.'

Social drinking without alcohol

If you don't want to drink alcohol, there are many other drinks to choose from and you can be inventive.

Fruit juices are great for you. They contain many vitamins and minerals to keep you healthy. All sorts are available, from exotic tropical juices to the standard orange and apple. You can experiment by mixing them or make them more exciting by adding fizzy soft drinks such as lemonade or soda.

There is a multitude of soft drinks, including canned and bottled fizzy drinks. Many 'pops' have a high sugar content, but you can avoid drinking too much sugar by choosing varieties labelled 'diet' or 'no added sugar'.

We all need water and most of us do not drink enough of it. We need it to clear toxins from our body. If we drink enough water, it makes us feel good and have fewer headaches and helps our skin and complexion. You can safely drink tap water or choose bottled or canned mineral waters. Some are even fruit-flavoured.

Milk is good for you too. It contains protein and lots of calcium, needed to keep your bones strong. You don't have to drink full fat milk and worry about the calories. Semi-skimmed and skimmed milk contain the same goodness and less fat. You can have fun inventing your own milk shakes, like Tom's 'mucky milk shake':

200 ml milk
1 scoop vanilla ice cream
1 banana
2 teaspoons of drinking
    chocolate
Blend until frothy.

You can also invent your own non-alcoholic cocktails, like those shown here. All these alternatives should help equip you to make the choice you want.

Strawberry whizz

fresh strawberries
1 can pineapple chunks
juice of half lemon
200 mls lemonade
Blend together till frothy. Serve in tall glasses with ice and drink with a straw.

Spice number

150 mls orange juice
150 mls apple juice
half teaspoon cinnamon powder
grated nutmeg
2 teaspoons honey
Warm the ingredients together in a saucepan. Drink warm, decorated with a lemon slice.

Silky delight

2 scoops of vanilla ice cream
1 can raspberries
150 mls cranberry juice
Blend the ice cream and raspberries together till smooth and frothy. Then add the cranberry juice and blend again. Serve in a tall glass, decorate with fresh raspberries or float a scoop of ice cream in it.

5 The medical problems
How alcohol damages health

Most people drink sensibly most of the time, and when small amounts of alcohol are drunk regularly there can actually be a health benefit (see page 16). But regularly drinking more than these sensible levels rapidly starts to damage health. It is estimated that in England and Wales 33,000 deaths per year can be attributed to alcohol.

Getting hooked

Alcohol is a mood-altering substance. It also alters the activity of many parts of the body. People who drink regularly develop a 'tolerance' to alcohol, which means that their sensitivity to it is reduced and they feel they need ever more alcohol to produce the same effect as before. They are also becoming 'dependent' on alcohol. This means that their body has got so used to regular alcohol consumption that there is a compulsion to keep consuming. The dependence is both physical and psychological.

Stereotype
We all have preconceived ideas of what someone is like who has been labelled 'alcoholic'.

A person dependent on alcohol rapidly develops withdrawal symptoms (see page 56) if they suddenly stop drinking. These symptoms are usually the opposite of the symptoms induced by alcohol. So, whereas alcohol slows down brain activity, in withdrawal the brain becomes overactive. The person may seem jumpy and shaky and may even have a convulsion or fit. Their heart rate will rise. They will feel sick and often vomit and have diarrhoea. The psychological part of dependence means that, if withdrawal occurs suddenly, the person craves, or feels a desperate need for, alcohol.

It is easy to recognize the extreme alcoholic, but there are many, many more people who have a degree of dependence on alcohol and who are drinking so much that alcohol is having a harmful effect on them. Many of these people do not see themselves as alcoholic or problem drinkers, despite the evidence.

Commonest cases

It is often thought that alcohol dependence is a problem of older people. However the peak age for alcohol dependence is between 16 and 24 years for both men and women.

Ben's Dad

Ben is 14. He's noticed a big change in his Dad recently. He knows that he's having problems at work. His Dad was a handsome man and used to like to keep fit. They went for runs together. But now Dad has put on weight. He always looks flushed and red in the face and goes on about how rotten he feels. It drives Mum mad. He's always saying he's tired or got a headache and using indigestion mixture because he feels sick or has belly ache. Ben has also noticed that he's not bothered going to work on a couple of occasions. He never seems to get home on time. His temper's always on a short fuse. Ben's suspicious that he's drinking. He's seen the evidence.

Doctors use different techniques to try to work out whether a patient's alcohol consumption may be hazardous to them. Alcohol excess could be contributing to almost any problem that a patient attends a doctor's surgery with. A simple technique that doctors can use is a questionnaire.

The CAGE questionnaire
- Have you ever felt you should Cut down on your drinking?
- Have people Annoyed you by criticizing your drinking?
- Have you ever felt bad or Guilty about your drinking?
- Have you ever had a drink first thing in the morning to steady your nerves or get rid of a hangover (Eye-opener)?

The MAST (Michigan Alcoholism Screening Test) questionnaire
- Do you feel you are a normal drinker?
- Do friends and relatives think you are a normal drinker?
- Have you ever attended a meeting of Alcoholics Anonymous?
- Have you ever lost friends or girlfriends/boyfriends because of drinking?
- Have you ever got into trouble at work because of drinking?
- Have you ever neglected your obligations, your family, or your work for two or more days in a row because you were drinking?
- Have you ever had delirium tremens, severe shaking, heard voices or hallucinated after heavy drinking?
- Have you ever gone to anyone for help about your drinking?
- Have you ever been in hospital because of drinking?
- Have you ever been arrested for drunk driving or driving after drinking?

'It can be difficult to get the truth about how much someone drinks. People are usually ashamed to confess it and do not really believe it could be causing some of the illnesses that they come with. Really, I should ask about alcohol with most of the problems I see.' (Dr Smith, family doctor)

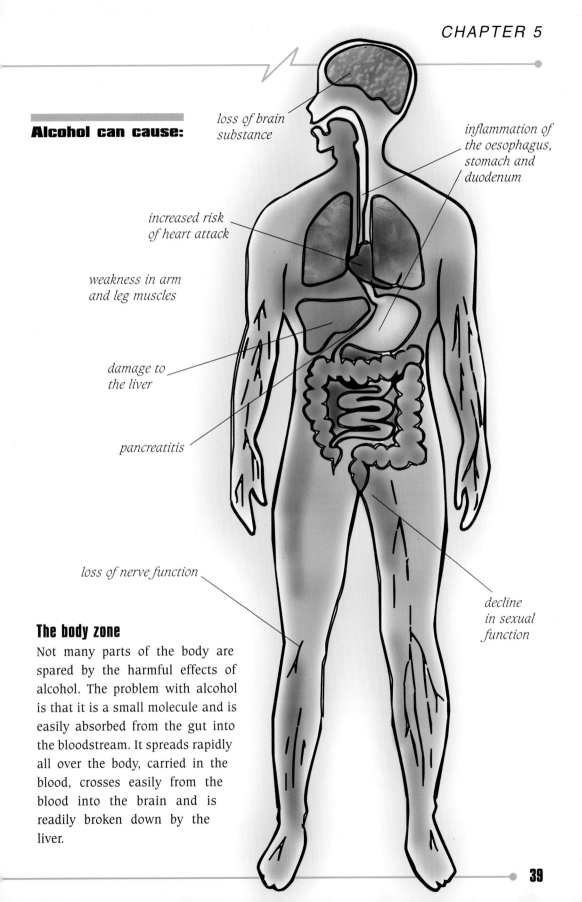

Alcohol can cause:

loss of brain substance

inflammation of the oesophagus, stomach and duodenum

increased risk of heart attack

weakness in arm and leg muscles

damage to the liver

pancreatitis

loss of nerve function

decline in sexual function

The body zone

Not many parts of the body are spared by the harmful effects of alcohol. The problem with alcohol is that it is a small molecule and is easily absorbed from the gut into the bloodstream. It spreads rapidly all over the body, carried in the blood, crosses easily from the blood into the brain and is readily broken down by the liver.

The digestive system

This includes all the gut from the mouth to the anus and other organs that assist in the digestion of food such as the liver and the pancreas. It is the first part of the body that alcohol hits.

Indigestion caused by inflammation in the gullet (oesophagus), stomach and first part of the small intestine (the duodenum) is much more common in people who drink heavily. This inflammation can progress and become ulcers, which may then bleed. Bleeding from the oesophagus and/or stomach is common, especially after alcohol binges. It is easy to tell when this is happening because the person will vomit blood and may collapse from blood loss.

The pancreas, which is involved in making digestive juices, can be harmed by alcohol. People with pancreatitis suffer repeated attacks of severe abdominal pain with diarrhoea and vomiting.

Inflammation in the gut and damage to the pancreas both affect the body's ability to absorb nutrients and so the problem drinker can become seriously malnourished and lacking in vital vitamins and minerals. Because alcohol itself is a rich source of energy, a person who is dependent on alcohol will probably drink instead of eating, so adding to the deficiencies they already have.

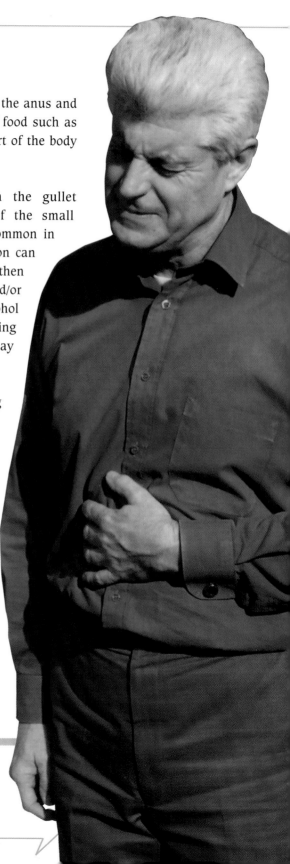

Indigestion
Heavy drinking can give you painful indigestion.

Sidney

Emma's grandfather, Sidney, is 69. Sadly he's in hospital now and it looks as though he hasn't long to live. The doctors say there is nothing further they can do. Sidney has drunk heavily for years. His wife, Lesley, died before Emma was born and that's when he turned to the bottle. He lost his job because of his drinking. After that his only pleasure was to go to the pub twice a day and drown his sorrows. Now he's paying the price. He has liver failure. You should see him. He's a shadow of his former self. His face is flushed and you can see little blood vessels like spiders all over his cheeks. He's lost so much weight that his face and chest look really wasted. But his belly is huge. The doctors say it's full of fluid. His liver is hard and uncomfortable. His blood isn't clotting properly, so he's covered in bruises and he's also vomited blood before now. As a result he has no energy. He's going a horrible yellow colour. He just seems to be lying there waiting to die.

Alcohol has a direct toxic effect on the liver. The first change to occur in the liver of a heavy drinker is the laying down of fat – 'fatty liver'. Alcohol damages the liver's ability to deal with fat normally. However, if the person stops drinking, this process of fatty change can be reversed.

The next change is 'alcoholic hepatitis', inflammation in the liver caused by the poisoning effect of alcohol. People with alcoholic hepatitis have a fever, abdominal pain and jaundice. Again it is possible for these changes to be reversed if the person stops drinking and the liver is allowed to recover.

The final and most serious liver change is cirrhosis of the liver. It seems to develop after many years of heavy drinking. Cirrhosis means that the liver tissue becomes scarred and the active cells of the liver are replaced by scar tissue. Cirrhosis of the liver can progress to liver failure where the liver is unable to fulfil any of its normal functions. It is inevitably fatal.

Liver damage

A healthy liver (top) carries out all its functions efficiently. But if the liver tissue is damaged (bottom), this vital organ may fail completely.

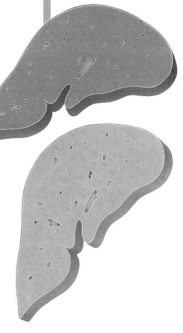

The heart, blood and blood vessels

As a toxic chemical, alcohol is harmful to the main blood-making factory in the body, the bone marrow.

The heart too can be damaged by alcohol. Many people who binge drink notice palpitations or a racing pulse after drinking. In the USA this is known as 'holiday heart' as most people binge drink on holiday or at weekends. This is a direct toxic effect of alcohol on the rhythm of the heart. Rarely, in people who abuse alcohol for many years, the heart muscle can be damaged. This is called alcoholic cardiomyopathy. In this condition the muscle does not pump efficiently and the heart starts to fail. It is an untreatable condition.

We have seen (page 16) that a small regular intake of alcohol can actually protect against high blood pressure, heart attacks and stroke. But once alcohol consumption exceeds that low level it starts to have the reverse effect. Blood pressure rises and the consequent risks of heart attack and stroke also increase.

Heart attack
A machine called a defibrillator is used to try to revive a heart attack victim.

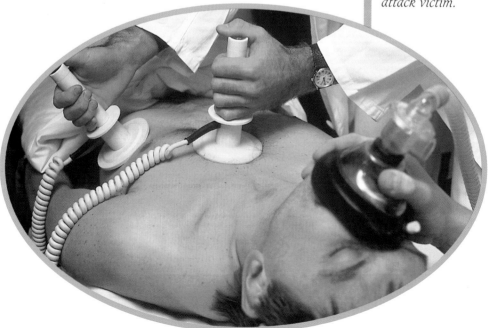

Brain scan
*When a patient's
head enters the scanning
machine, an image of their
brain appears on the computer screen.*

The brain and nervous system

People who drink alcohol to excess for long periods of time are at risk of developing any number of problems involving the brain and nerves. Alcohol also seems to be directly toxic to nervous tissue – neurotoxic. Brain scans of alcoholics often show cerebral atrophy or loss of brain substance. This can cause subtle problems in brain function, such as the ability to plan or organize one's life. Commonly, when the brain has been damaged by alcohol, the balance centre known as the cerebellum is attacked. This can be recognized in alcoholics because they become unsteady, with poor balance and coordination. They develop shaky hands and often have slurred, stuttering speech.

Nerves and muscles are also attacked by alcohol, leading to weakness of the muscles in the arms and legs and pins and needles in the hands and feet. These can be very debilitating and make people feel tired and uncomfortable.

Enrique

Enrique lived in LA. He was in with a bad gang. He'd been drinking for many years and it was said that he had started getting into heavier stuff. Anyway, life was pretty bad for him. His girlfriend had just dumped him. He just went out and apparently got very drunk. The next thing anyone knew was that he was found in his Dad's car in the garage, with a pipe taking the exhaust back into the car. He was dead from asphyxiation. He left no suicide note. I reckon, if he hadn't been drunk, he may have thought twice about what he was doing.

As far as the effect of alcohol on the mind is concerned, it can be difficult to separate cause and effect. Do people with psychiatric problems drink to feel better or do people who drink excessively suffer psychiatric side effects?

We know that alcohol depresses brain activity. This slowing down often makes people who drink too much too often feel low and sad. Suicide is a common consequence of this. About 1 per cent of people who are seriously dependent on alcohol end up committing suicide. Furthermore, problems with alcohol and other dependence-inducing substances contribute to up to 50 per cent of suicides in 15-24 year-olds, according to a US study.

The crippling psychiatric illness of schizophrenia causes frightening and bewildering thoughts in individuals who suffer from it. They often have delusions and hallucinations. Alcohol is often used by people with this illness to try to suppress the worrying thoughts. Equally, alcohol in excess can mimic some of the symptoms of schizophrenia, again inducing delusions.

The big C

Excess alcohol consumption increases cancer risk.

⦿ *It doubles the risk of cancer of the gullet.*

⦿ *It trebles the risk of cancer of the throat.*

⦿ *It quadruples the risk of cancer of the voice box.*

Alcohol and fertility, sexual function and pregnancy

In men, drinking heavily has many effects on sexual function. It is often difficult to achieve or sustain an erection when drunk. With long-term over-indulgence in alcohol, sperm production in the testes is reduced, the testes may shrink and levels of the male hormone testosterone fall.

Women who drink excessively also suffer effects on sexual function and fertility. Periods become irregular. Fertility can be reduced by the direct toxic effect of alcohol on the ovaries.

Heavy drinking during pregnancy can interrupt the normal development of the baby in the womb. Babies can be born with the fetal alcohol syndrome. These babies are very small, they have an odd facial appearance and brain development is also damaged. Regular alcohol consumption through pregnancy may also have more subtle effects on the development of the infant and may contribute to the child having learning difficulties later.

Fetal alcohol syndrome
This little boy was born with the fetal alcohol syndrome. His adoptive parents provide for his complex care needs.

6 The social harm
Alcohol's effects on families and society

Alcohol dependence and drunkenness don't just harm the health of problem drinkers. They have a harmful effect on the drinkers' families and on wider society too.

The domestic scene

A frightening statistic states that nearly a million children in the UK could be living in a family where an adult has an alcohol problem. Sharing a home with someone who regularly drinks to excess or is frequently drunk can alter your life forever.

'Dad is either drunk or hung-over and usually out at the pub. Mum left a couple of years ago. I often get hit when Dad is having one of his tempers. Then he goes all soft and cries and apologises. He just forgets to bother with us.'
(Kevin, 12)

An adult with a drinking problem (an alcoholic) needs frequent 'top-ups' of alcohol. As tolerance develops, they will drink more and more and may have episodes of drunkenness. Since alcohol reduces people's inhibitions, the drunk person may behave bizarrely, say or do things that they later regret and become violent. The physical health of the alcoholic will deteriorate the more they drink.

Often their drinking pattern makes them feel guilty about their behaviour. The guilt drives them to conceal the reality and pretend to themselves and to others that they do not have a problem. Guilt also makes them feel low and fed up and this can progress to depression and even suicidal thoughts. All these negative feelings have a bad effect on

'Mum's been hitting the bottle for a couple of years. I know, although Dad tries to cover up for her. She's scared of his posh work do's, so has to have a drink first. Now she needs a drink before she does anything. I can't go to her with any of my problems.'
(Jane, 15)

Family problems

Many types of problem are commoner in families with an alcoholic member or are contributed to by alcohol.

- Domestic violence – 40 per cent of incidents are influenced by alcohol.
- Family breakdown – 30 per cent of divorces are said to have alcohol as a factor.
- Child abuse – 20 per cent of cases are influenced by alcohol.
- Domestic accidents – 33 per cent are influenced by alcohol.
- Financial insecurity.
- Unemployment.

relationships. The alcoholic becomes dishonest with their partner and possibly abusive both physically and verbally. Their sexual relationship often falls apart. Money is spent on alcohol and not on the needs of the family.

Families work well when certain features are consistent. Individuals within a family fulfil different roles, such as earning money, cooking, doing the washing, driving, being involved in sport, helping with homework and so on. Many roles are shared. Life works

Violence
It's especially frightening for children to see their father drunk and violent.

better if we stick to what we do well rather than behaving irrationally. An alcoholic parent may be able to achieve good parenting at times but lets it fall apart at others. This behaviour can make children feel very insecure.

'There was no routine. Our birthdays were often forgotten. We rarely sat down together for meals. Sometimes there wasn't even food in the house.' (Sarah)

Homes should be safe and happy places. Life with an alcoholic is often chaotic and can be violent. The alcoholic cannot be relied on, may forget to attend special events that were promised and may spend so much on drink that other family pleasures have to be missed. The alcoholic parent can be very self-centred and ignore the emotional needs of others.

Zak

Zak is 14. His Dad is violent and aggressive and frequently drunk. His Mum doesn't recognize the problem and cowers in front of his Dad, not standing up to him. Home is chaotic.

For years, Zak avoided having friends back home. And, since he could never predict his parents' response to things, he always refused invitations to other people's houses. Now he just stays out. Nobody seems to notice whether he's home or not. So, he either hangs out with an older bunch of lads or takes his skateboard down to the skate park and stays there until late.

When he was little, he was often bullied because his Mum never organized decent clothes for school or getting his hair cut. He never had many friends. Now he's with the gang of older lads, he thinks it's cool to have a go at the younger kids at school. He was expelled from his last school for slashing someone's clothes with a knife. He's always getting in trouble for fighting.

His school work is hopeless. To get attention, he disrupts classes and is always getting punishments. Even if he gets in trouble, his Mum and Dad don't seem to care. People at school, his form tutor and the school counsellor, have tried to work with him but he doesn't trust them. Surely they can see it's not his fault and do something about it. But they don't seem to care either.

Sometimes, he just really hates himself and can't see much point in life. He goes and sits alone on a park bench. He thinks, maybe it's all his fault that his Dad is so useless. Perhaps, if he had been better at football or got good marks at school, Dad would have noticed. He has actually got hold of some vodka on occasions to try to drown his own sorrows.

The survivors

Certain factors can help protect you if you live in a family that is dysfunctional because of alcohol. Children are more likely to survive unharmed by the experience if:

- there is one parent who is strong and supportive and can hold the family together
- they have a loving and supportive relationship with an adult outside the family who can then be relied on
- they have a strong and resilient personality
- the rest of the family have managed to steer clear of the disruption caused by the alcoholic
- they do more and more outside the family, building their own life with success at school or in sport or some other hobby.

Drink-driving

In the USA in 1998, 15,935 lives were lost in alcohol-related motor crashes. This accounted for 35 per cent of all traffic fatalities. In the UK, in the last ten years, the number of drink-driving fatalities has decreased by 56 per cent, and the proportion of drivers testing positive to alcohol on breath tests has fallen from 42 per cent to 14 per cent. However, that figure is not continuing to fall and there is no room for complacency.

The maximum level of blood alcohol that is permitted for driving in the UK is 80mg/100 ml. An adult man can reach this blood level with just 4 units of alcohol (2 pints of beer) and an adult woman with just 3 units. We also know that judgement is already impaired with a blood alcohol level of 60 mg/100 ml. Remembering that alcohol has a faster and more significant effect on inexperienced young drinkers, it is not surprising

Breathalyser

The breathalyser is used at the roadside to test for alcohol in the breath of drivers.

Alcohol-related accidents

Many surveys are carried out into the number of accidents that are alcohol-related. A review of surveys from throughout the English-speaking world showed that the following percentages of types of accidents were alcohol-related:

- *50 per cent of head injuries*
- *13-37 per cent of non-fatal falls*
- *21-47 per cent of drownings*
- *9-68 per cent of deaths from burns*
- *35 per cent of accidents at work*
- *14 per cent of all road accidents*
- *30 per cent of accidents involving pedestrians*
- *20-30 per cent overall of all types of accidents*

that the ability to drive safely is more quickly impaired in young drivers. It was found that nearly half of the drivers killed in alcohol-related accidents were under 25 years old.

'Jim was going to drive home but he was definitely over the limit. I just took his keys and called a taxi.' (Beth, 18)

However, young people also hold strong opinions about drink-driving. In a British survey of young people, the majority supported tougher measures to control drink-driving. 70 per cent said they would drink no alcohol if they were going to drive. 66 per cent said they would make sure that one individual in a group was nominated as driver and the others would make sure this individual did not drink. They had strategies to stop someone who had been drinking from driving.

Many felt that the police should be able to stop people at random to breath-test them. Along with this, many felt the drink-drive alcohol limit should be lowered. Tougher penalties were also thought to be a good idea.

Drunk-drivers

In New York State, USA, convicted drunk-drivers must attend a series of meetings where people who have lost loved ones in drunk-driving accidents tell their stories.

Alcohol in the workplace

People in some jobs are more likely to become problem drinkers. Obviously, those with easy access to alcohol, such as bar tenders, are at risk. People in high-stress jobs who work alone, such as doctors and dentists, are also at risk of turning to alcohol.

Alcohol and work do not mix. Drinking at work has a significant effect on how we perform. Concentration is impaired. The ability to operate machinery safely is reduced. Drinking at home also influences the ability to work normally. It is a common cause of absenteeism and reduced efficiency. It is claimed that excessive drinking costs Britain £3.3 billion a year, mostly through sick leave, unemployment and premature death.

Drunkenness and violent crime

It is a criminal offence to be drunk and disorderly in a public place. There is also a link between alcohol and the crimes of vandalism, hooliganism and assault. Violence is often linked with consumption of alcohol, although it can be difficult to say which is cause and effect.

When groups of individuals get together, their behaviour can become unrestrained. If alcohol is also involved, the situation can get out of hand faster.

Facial injuries

In the UK in 1997, there were 50,000 assaults involving facial injuries to young people aged 15-25. 61 per cent of these were alcohol-related.

Policing

We have had to investigate our policing policy. It was becoming obvious that young people's drinking, especially at the weekend, was causing significant public disturbance – noise, intimidation and so on. There were increasing episodes of vandalism. Then there was a knifing outside the pub. There was a public outcry. Now we have CCTV monitoring and a greater police presence especially at closing time. It's a fine balance allowing people to have a good time but also preventing disorder and injury. (PC Wilson, local community policeman)

Street drinkers

It seems that a high proportion of people sleeping rough have alcohol problems. Many of these people are socially isolated. Many may have become homeless because of other problems, such as psychiatric illness. Their alcohol dependence may have been the cause of their homelessness or may have developed as a result of sleeping rough.

Alcohol and violence

According to the British Crime Survey, in 1998, 41 per cent of all people committing violence were under the influence of alcohol. This was broken down into:

- *stranger violence. A high proportion of assaults committed by a stranger to the victim occur near pubs and clubs. 53 per cent of assailants were under the influence of alcohol.*
- *violent assaults committed by someone acquainted with the victim. 43 per cent of such assailants were under the influence of alcohol.*
- *domestic violence. 32 per cent of assailants were under the influence of alcohol.*

7 Help is at hand
Prevention, self-help and medical treatment

What can individuals and societies do to lessen the occurrence of alcoholism? And what treatments are available for problem drinkers?

Preventing the problem

The most basic way of addressing the problem of alcohol dependence in a population is to try to prevent it occurring. Societies use the following methods to try to reduce alcohol consumption and encourage sensible drinking:

- increasing taxation on alcohol and the cost of drinks
- imposing purchasing restrictions – for example, increasing the legal age limit for purchasing alcohol. In the USA this age limit has recently been raised to 21 years. There is some evidence that this has reduced the number of alcohol-related deaths in the under-21 age group.
- restricting licences – for instance, removing the licence to sell alcohol from premises where drunken behaviour and under-age drinking occur regularly
- labelling the alcohol content of drinks more clearly so that people can make an informed choice
- labelling drinks with health warnings
- restricting alcohol consumption, e.g. at work or at sporting events
- providing education in school about the effects of alcohol
- running health promotion campaigns regarding the risks and benefits of alcohol.

Education
High-school students listen to a talk about alcohol and drug abuse.

For an individual, the best way of reducing the risk of any problem with alcohol is to stay below the recommended drinking levels (see page 20).

Help for a moderate problem

People whose drinking already puts them at a moderate risk of health damage can still take control of their consumption. Understanding the risks and being aware of the benefits of cutting down will probably help their motivation to do so. If you are someone with a moderate problem, one of the first steps to help yourself is to keep a diary of your drinking.

The next task is to look at your drinking and draw up a balance sheet.

Mr Jones' Diary

	what and when	where	with whom
Monday	2 pints of beer	pub	with mates
	3 glasses of wine	at home	with the wife
	in the evening		
Tuesday	same	same	same
Wednesday	none		
Thursday	none		
Friday	4 pints beer	pub	with work mates
	1 glass wine	at home	with friends
Saturday	1 bottle of wine	at home	with friends
	and 2 brandies		
	with dinner		
Sunday	2 pints beer	pub	brother
	at lunch		
	3 glasses wine	at home	family
	with dinner		

Mr Jones' total is 38 units per week

Balance Sheet	
I feel good with a drink	Regretting my behaviour
It keeps me in with friends	Feeling awful the next day
Good fun	Being taken advantage of when drunk
Pub is the only place to go out	Vomiting
I dance better with a drink	Hangover

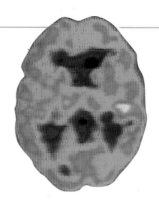

Then you can look at strategies that will improve the situation without removing all the pleasure from drinking. Here are some tips:

- Cut down the number of drinks per day.
- Drink lower-alcohol alternatives or alternate alcoholic with non-alcoholic drinks.
- Have alcohol-free days.
- Make each drink last longer.
- Get others to help you. Tell them you are cutting down.
- Find other ways to relax.

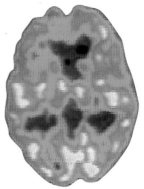

Treatment for a heavy drinker at high risk of harm

This person is probably addicted to alcohol, has developed tolerance so that they are drinking more to get the same effect, and will have withdrawal symptoms if they stop drinking. They will probably need medical help to withdraw from alcohol. This withdrawal is known as detoxification. Sometimes the risk of severe problems with withdrawal is so high that the patient has to be detoxified

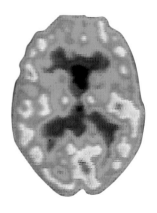

Withdrawal symptoms

tremors	insomnia
muscle jerks	nightmares
faster heart rate	anxiety
higher temperature	major and minor convulsions
higher blood pressure	delirium tremens or DTs =
hyperventilation	hallucinations, impaired
poor appetite	memory, disorientation,
nausea and vomiting	agitation
diarrhoea	

These symptoms can last for 3-5 days and start 6-24 hours after the last drink.

Withdrawal and the brain

In these scans of cross-sections of the brain, 10 days, 20 days and 30 days after withdrawal from alcohol, the yellow shows brain activity.

in a special hospital detoxification unit. Usually a tranquillizer such as diazepam is given to slow down brain activity again as alcohol is withdrawn. Medication can also be given to reduce some of the other withdrawal symptoms like vomiting and diarrhoea.

'It was horrible!
I didn't sleep for two nights. It felt
as though my heart would stop beating. My
throat felt as if it was closing. I was vomiting and
shaking and having hot and cold sweats.
It all lasted about 3 days.'
(Jackie)

Maintaining abstinence and rehabilitation

In many ways, withdrawal is the easy part of stopping drinking. Much more difficult is staying off alcohol. Many alcoholics relapse many times before they achieve their goal of abstinence. They need to be highly motivated and well-supported to stay off alcohol.

Praise and encouragement from family and friends will help them keep going. If your friend is staying off alcohol, help them to avoid circumstances that may be too tempting, like going out to the pub, and reduce their access to alcohol by socializing at alcohol-free venues. Help them to avoid the stresses that may turn them back to drink and find other ways of dealing with stress such as relaxation or exercise.

Professionals can offer other types of support.

- Counselling can be provided by local drug and alcohol services. These may be linked to psychiatric services or may be run by charities. The counselling can take many forms, including group therapy, behavioural therapy, social skills training and stress management.

- Medication can be used to help to prevent relapse. Many different drugs are used for this purpose, including Disulfiram or Antabuse, Naltrexone and Acamprosate. Antabuse works by giving the patient severe side effects within 20 minutes of drinking alcohol. These include nausea, flushing and diarrhoea. Naltrexone appears to increase control over alcoholic urges and helps the person to resist thoughts about drinking. Acamprosate reduces craving and alcohol consumption by its direct effect on the brain.

⊚ Supportive treatments include alternative therapies such as acupuncture and hypnosis. These can help the person to relax and reduce cravings.

Self-help groups are commonly used and recommended to assist recovering alcoholics to stay off drink. Alcoholics Anonymous is the most well-known. It is a worldwide organization. All it requires of anyone who wants its support is a desire to stop drinking. It is not allied with any religious group, political organization or institution.

The ethos of AA is that a more experienced AA member who has themselves conquered alcoholism sponsors a new member. The experienced member helps the new member to attend AA groups regularly and to work through what are called the 12 steps of recovery. These include

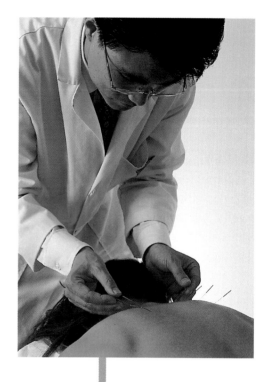

Acupuncture
Some people find acupuncture helpful in dealing with dependency problems.

AA meeting
In an AA group, all participants suffer alcohol problems and they all support each other in their recovery.

- admitting that they have no control over alcohol
- being prepared to examine themselves critically
- commitment to honesty and humility
- accepting the reality of their past
- accepting the harm they have caused
- taking responsibility for repairing the harm done.

'Jan found attending and talking at the AA group very hard at first. We had to reassure her that we had all been where she was, that none of us are perfect but are all there to help each other. We have to support each other through relapses too.'

Help for family and friends

Al-Anon and Alateen are sister organizations to Alcoholics Anonymous. They too are worldwide organizations which offer a self-help and recovery programme for families and friends of alcoholics. You can get help from these organizations even if your alcoholic relative does not recognize their problem and is not receiving treatment. Alateen runs support groups specifically for teenagers.

There are some important points to remember if you are struggling and living with an alcoholic.

1. You cannot control your parent's drinking. It is not your fault.

2. You are not alone. There are many other children and young people living with alcoholics.

3. You can talk to someone about the problem. There are helplines and organizations for you to talk to and meet other young people who are suffering similarly.

4. Don't feel guilty or ashamed. Your parent's drinking is a disease.

5. Don't try to hide your parent's drinking problem or think that you can cure them. They have to seek help themselves.

6. Find fun things to do outside the home. You are still allowed to enjoy yourself. Joining clubs can give you enjoyment and be supportive.

Six 'C's to help you

You did not CAUSE it.

You cannot CONTROL it.

You cannot CURE it.

You can take CARE of yourself.

You can COMMUNICATE your feelings.

You can make healthy CHOICES.

Resources

CHILDLINE
Telephone counselling service for any young person with concerns about themselves or others.

Freephone: 0800 1111

DRINKLINE
Government-sponsored helpline.

Freephone: 0800 917 8282

AL-ANON and ALATEEN
These are branches of the same organization that offers support to family and friends of those with an alcohol problem. Alateen is specifically for young people.

Telephone: 020 7403 0888

Website: www.hexnet.co.uk/alanon/

AA (ALCOHOLICS ANONYMOUS)
Support organization for people with an alcohol problem.

Stonebow House,
Stonebow,
York YO1 2NJ

National helpline: 0845 7697 555

Website: www.aa-uk.org.uk

National Association for Children of Alcoholics (NACOA)
P. O. Box 64,
Fishponds,
Bristol BS16 2UH

Telephone: 0800 289061

Website: www.nacoa.demon.co.uk/kidskit. html

ALCOHOL CONCERN
275 Gray's Inn Road,
London WC1X 8QF

Telephone: 020 7928 7377

Website: www.alcoholconcern.org.uk

Contains a series of information fact sheets such as:

Alcohol and UK Law
Young People and Alcohol

Also contains *Alcohol Services Directory* for information about local alcohol services.

Website
An NHS Health Promotion website designed for young people is called:

Think about drink – www.wrecked.co.uk

Publications

Useful guides available from Alcohol Concern include:

A Guide for Teenagers

A Woman's Guide to Alcohol (published by Alcohol Concern)
A short booklet answering the questions many women ask about alcohol.

Enough Bottle (published by Alcohol Concern)

Let's drink to your health! A self-help guide to sensible drinking, by I. Robertson and N. Heather (published by the British Psychological Society, 1986)

Say when! Everything a woman needs to know about alcohol and drinking problems by R Kent (published by Sheldon Press, 1989)

Say When – How much is too much? (published by Alcohol Concern and the Health Education Authority)

Think About Drink – Alcohol and health: all you need to know

The following are available from Al-Anon:

Courage to be Me

If your parents drink too much

Hope for Children of Alcoholics: Alateen

What's Drunk, Mummy?

Glossary

%abv	percentage of alcohol by volume of a drink.
alcohol	a chemical properly known as ethanol, made by the fermentation of sugar.
alcohol dependence	a state of dependence on alcohol identified by the fact that withdrawal symptoms occur when the person stops drinking.
alcohol intoxication	poisoning by drinking large volumes of alcohol at one time.
alcopops	alcoholic lemonades, colas and fizzy pops.
binge drinking	drinking large volumes of alcohol on single occasions.
craving for alcohol	a feeling of compulsion to keep drinking.
detoxification	controlled withdrawal from alcohol with supportive help.
distillation	means of strengthening the concentration of alcohol in a drink.
drunkenness	over-consumption of alcohol to the point where control is lost.
hangover	the after-effect of drinking too much alcohol, characterized by headache, dry mouth and irritability.

hypothermia	condition when the body's temperature falls too low.
intoxicating substance	something that is toxic or poisonous to us.
licensed premises	places such as bars that posses a licence to allow them to sell alcohol.
mood-altering substance	a substance that alters brain chemistry to change the way we feel.
problem drinker	a person whose drinking habit is causing problems in their life.
standard drink	a measure used in the USA to compare drinks of similar strength.
teetotal	drinking no alcohol.
tolerance to alcohol	reduced sensitivity to alcohol, such that the person needs to drink more to achieve the same effect.
units of alcohol	measures used to compare drinks of similar strength.
withdrawal symptoms	the symptoms someone gets if they stop drinking suddenly.

Index

Note

Photographs illustrating the case studies in this book were posed by models.